QUICK ACCESS®

CALIFORNIA
SOUTH CENTRAL COAST
WINE COUNTRY

FEATURING PHOTOGRAPHY
BY
WILLIAM G. HARTSHORN

CONTENTS

PHOTO CREDITS

Photography by William G. Hartshorn
www.WGHartshorn.com

Photography by Maxine Hesse:
Pages 10, 28-29, 31, 33-34, 49-50, 52-53, 76-77, 94
Pages 13 (bottom) 72-73 Courtesy of The Dunes Center
Photography by Daryl Weisser (DWImages@aol.com) Page 64

Wine information courtesy of:

Pages 38-39 The Wine Institute www.wineinstitute.org
Pages 42-43 Santa Barbara Vintners Assn www.sbcountywines.com
Pages 68-69, 75 San Luis Obispo Vintners Assn www.slowine.com
Pages 77,83-84 Paso Robles Wine Country Alliance www.pasowine.com

For winery locations, see Global Graphics'
**"QUICK ACCESS® SANTA BARBARA, SAN LUIS OBISPO, PASO ROBLES
WINE COUNTRY MAP and GUIDE"**

IMPRESSUM

PUBLISHED BY
© 2006 *global graphics*, Oceanside CA
www.globalgraphicsmaps.com
Cover design & layout: Phil Timper
www.timperarts.com

Printed in Singapore

INTRODUCTION

Although California's "wine country" is synonymous with the Napa-Sonoma region, the area from San Miguel down to Santa Barbara is definitely the 'up and coming' wine country. The Edna Valley, Santa Maria Valley and Santa Ynez Valley wines have earned accolades since the 1970s-1980s and do so continually as the wine industry there continues to expand.

Cold winds bite through the east-west valley surrounding the Santa Rita Hills region of California's South Central Coast. Up until the late 1960s, grape growers primarily sold their crops to the wineries of the Napa and Sonoma Valleys. At that point in time, regional vintners started to realize they should process their own grapes locally. Pioneers such as Sanford Winery and Babcock Vineyards began to bottle Pinot Noir. Other wineries soon sprung up, such as Foley Estates, Fiddlehead, Santa Barbary Winery, Clos Pepe and Fess Parker, to name a few.

COASTAL WINE COUNTRY

California vintners, although respectful of European winemaking traditions, do not necessarily adhere to the same techniques. They may use different types of wooden barrels for aging than do the Europeans. The taste of a Chardonnay wine, for example, may vary greatly between Northern California wineries and those elsewhere in the State, depending on whether they choose American oak or French oak barrels. Moreover "terroir" is an essential factor in grape growing, so the earth in which the grapes thrive has a significant influence on the final product.

This book is not intended for the oenophile (wine connoisseur), rather the focus is on the basics of enjoying wines, and a bit of knowledge makes the enjoyment richer. The major grape varietals grown in the region, in order of popularity, are:

CHARDONNAY wines are reminiscent of citrus fruits, pears, peaches, pineapple, sometimes spicy, sometimes like honey, butter or hazelnuts, ranging from dry to a buttery character. A favorite wine for its high crop yield, it is consistently rich and complex.

PINOT NOIR are full-bodied, rich wines with taste of berries or black cherry and tend to be lighter than cabernets and merlots. Sometimes there are notes of herbs or roses, raspberries, plums, spices, and flowers such as lavender, violets or jasmine.

SYRAH has deep color, is robust, full-bodied and high in tannins, giving it strong pepper, cinnamon, anise nuances as well as black raspberry, plum and currrant flavors. It is easier to grow than most other red wine grapes.

MERLOT ranges from a soft-bodied (lighter than Cabernet) wine with black cherry and currant flavor, to a medium-bodied wine of velvety smoothness, somewhat heavier than Cabernet. As it ages, Merlot may become "softer" with the tannins being less notable.

CABERNET SAUVIGNON is full-bodied with raspberry or currant, black cherry, plum and spice flavors with some overtones from oak barrels with high tannins. Colors are dark purple, with solid acidity. 'Cabs' aged in French or American oak barrels pick up woody, toasty or vanilla flavors in the slow oxidation process of barrel aging.

Winemaking involves the following basic steps:

Harvesting often is done early in the morning, thus keeping the grapes cool to avoid excessive color from the skins going into the juice. Crews of pickers line the fields using their sharp knives to cut each cluster from the vines.

Crushing must take place soon after picking of the grapes. Crush machines are set to remove each grape stem and to avoid breaking the bitter seeds inside the grape. Often two sets of crushers are used for red and white wines, avoiding color problems with white wines. An average winery crusher can process about 40 tons per hour, yielding 60-70 cases of wine.

Pressing is an alternative to crushing. Treading on the grapes, though a romantic notion, is no longer legal in the U.S. The weight of grapes in the vat released "free-run" juice, but then the more pressure applied by the press, the more juice is gathered. Too much pressure may give the juice unwanted flavor compounds, or harsh and bitter flavors. Presses have evolved from a wooden slat structure, to a small-volume "basket" type, then to a "bladder" press and since the 1980s to a "tank" press. Wineries thatgive tours explain which type they prefer.

Fermentation is a natural process which changes the sweet juice into alcohol and carbon dioxide through the action of yeast, other microflora, and sugar. The yeast metabolizes the sugar, thus converting the juice into carbon dioxide and ethanol (an alcohol). There are many methods of fermentation as well as many types of yeasts and temperature controls, but the results should be an enjoyable wine.

Clarifying removes visible and invisible particles from the wine, including spent yeast cells, proteins, tannins and grape skins. Either by racking, filtering, fining or centrifuging, the wines are rendered clear, bright and appetizing. The process also helps avoid potential dangers in the bottling process.

Aging is often done in wooden barrels primarily to make the wine smoother and softer. Red wines are aged more often than white wines in order to diminish the taste of tannins and bitter flavors typical in young reds. Wood aging emphasizes the origin of the wood (usually American or French oak or Califorina redwood). However, not all wines need be aged very long nor in wood. Many wines are bottled only a few weeks after harvest, after having spent that time in stainless-steel tanks. Some vintners use tanks at first, then place smaller batches of wine in wooden barrels to further refine the wines.

Blending of varietals is increasingly popular, and many are based on European combinations. Vintners will take, for example, Cabernet Sauvignon, Cabernet Franc and Merlot to make a Bordeau-style named "Meritage", achieving an unique taste. They may also blend from various vintages and/or vineyards.

Bottling today is done in ultra-modern, sanitary and sterile conditions to prevent yeast particles or bacterium from entering the bottles. Corks from an oak species grown in Spain and Portugal have traditionally been used, however plastic corks and screw-tops are gaining favor.

Labeling - catching the consumer's eye is very important and label designers enjoy a good business. The U.S. Federal government stipulates that bottles indicate type of wine, alcohol content, fluid contents, brand name and address and the area from which the grapes originate.

Distributing goes through many channels, including winery and regional tasting rooms, wholesale distributors, restaurant sales, wine clubs and Internet sales, particularly important for small "boutique wineries".

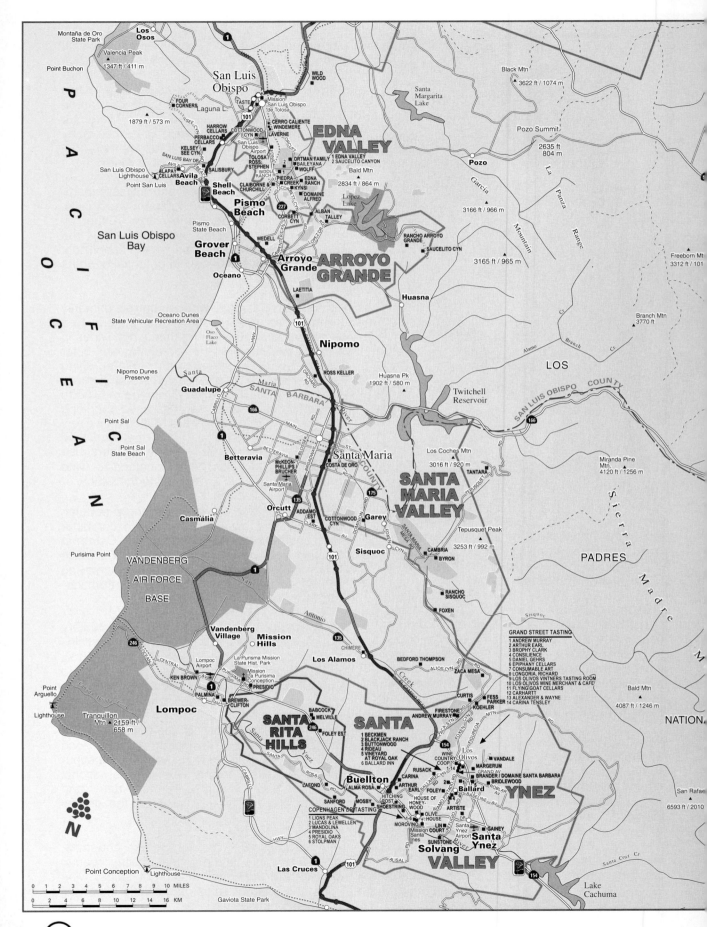

Montaña de Oro State Park
Los Osos
Valencia Peak 1347 ft / 411 m
Point Buchon
San Luis Obispo
WILD WOOD
Black Mtn 3622 ft / 1074 m
Santa Margarita Lake
Laguna L.
FOUR CORNERS
TASTE
Mission San Luis Obispo de Tolosa
CERRO CALIENTE
WINDEMERE
EDNA VALLEY
Pozo Summit
1879 ft / 573 m
HARROW CELLARS
COTTONWOOD CYN
LAVERNE
2635 ft 804 m
Pozo
PERBACCO CELLARS
San Luis Obispo Airport
ORTMAN FAMILY
BAILEYANA WOLFF
1 EDNA VALLEY
2 SAUCELITO CANYON
Garcia
KELSEY SEE CYN
TOLOSA ROSS STEPHEN
2
Bald Mtn 2834 ft / 864 m
La Panza Range
San Luis Obispo Lighthouse
SALISBURY
PIEDRA CREEK
EDNA RANCH
ALAPAY CELLARS
Avila Beach
BIDDLE RANCH RD
KYNSI
DOMAINE ALFRED
Mountain
Point San Luis
Shell Beach
CLAIBORNE & CHURCHILL
Lopez Lake
3166 ft / 966 m
3165 ft / 965 m
Freeborn Mtn 3312 ft / 101
Pismo Beach
CORBETT CYN
ALBAN
TALLEY
RANCHO ARROYO GRANDE
Pismo State Beach
WEDELL
SAUCELITO CYN
San Luis Obispo Bay
Grover Beach
Arroyo Grande
ARROYO GRANDE
Oceano
LAETITIA
Huasna
Oceano Dunes State Vehicular Recreation Area
Oso Flaco Lake
Nipomo
LOS
Nipomo Dunes Preserve
Santa
ROSS KELLER
Huasna Pk 1902 ft / 580 m
Twitchell Reservoir
Branch Mtn 3770 ft
Guadalupe
SANTA BARBARA
Maria
River
SAN LUIS OBISPO COUNTY
Alamo
Branch
Point Sal
CABRILLO
Betteravia
BETTERAVIA
Los Coches Mtn 3016 ft / 920 m
Miranda Pine Mtn. 4120 ft / 1256 m
Point Sal State Beach
McKEON PHILLIPS BRUCHER
MAIN
Santa Maria
COSTA DE ORO
TANTARA
Santa Maria Airport
SANTA MARIA VALLEY
Sierra Madre
Purisima Point
Casmalia
Orcutt
ADDAMO EST
COTTONWOOD CYN
Garey
PADRES
VANDENBERG AIR FORCE BASE
CLARK
Sisquoc
CAMBRIA
BYRON
Tepusquet Peak 3253 ft / 992 m
Bald Mtn 4087 ft / 1246 m
San
RANCHO SISQUOC
FOXEN
Antonio
135
CHIMERE
BEDFORD THOMPSON
ALIOS CYN
ZACA MESA
GRAND STREET TASTING
1 ANDREW MURRAY
2 ARTHUR EARL
3 BROPHY CLARK
4 CONSILIENCE
5 DANIEL GEHRS
6 EPIPHANY CELLARS
7 CONSUMABLE ART
8 LONGORIA, RICHARD
9 LOS OLIVOS VINTNERS TASTING ROOM
10 LOS OLIVOS WINE MERCHANT & CAFE
11 FLYING GOAT CELLARS
12 CARHARTT
13 ALEXANDER & WAYNE
14 CARINA TENSLEY
Point Arguello
Vandenberg Village
Mission Hills
Los Alamos
CURTIS
FESS PARKER
KOEHLER
Lighthouse
Lompoc Airport
La Purisima Mission State Hist. Park
FIRESTONE
ANDREW MURRAY
San Rafae 6593 ft / 2010
KEN BROWN
Mission La Purisima Conception
PRESIDIO
VANDALE
PALMINA
BREWER-CLIFTON
BABCOCK
MELVILLE
FOLEY EST
SANTA
Los Olivos
MARGERUM
BRANDER / DOMAINE SANTA BARBARA
BRIDLEWOOD
Tranquillon Mtn 2159 ft / 658 m
Lompoc
SANTA RITA HILLS
1 BECKMEN
2 BLACKJACK RANCH
3 BUTTONWOOD
4 RIDEAU
5 VINEYARD AT ROYAL OAK
6 BALLARD INN
WINE COUNTRY COOP
RUSACK
CARINA
ARTHUR EARL
FOLEY
Ballard
YNEZ
Buellton
ALMA ROSA
HITCHING POST
HOUSE OF HONEY-WOOD
ARTISTE
LAFOND
SANFORD
MOSBY
SHOESTRING
COPENHAGEN DRY TASTING
1 LIONS PEAK
2 LUCAS & LEWELLEN
3 MANDOLINA
4 PRESIDIO
5 ROYAL OAKS
6 STOLPMAN
OLIVE HOUSE
MOROVINO
LIN
Santa Ynez Airport
GAINEY
SUNSTONE
Santa Ines
Mission COURT
Solvang
Santa Ynez
Point Conception
Lighthouse
Las Cruces
VALLEY
Santa Cruz Cr
Lake Cachuma
Gaviota State Park

0 1 2 3 4 5   10 MILES
0 2 4 6 8 10 12 14 16 KM

N

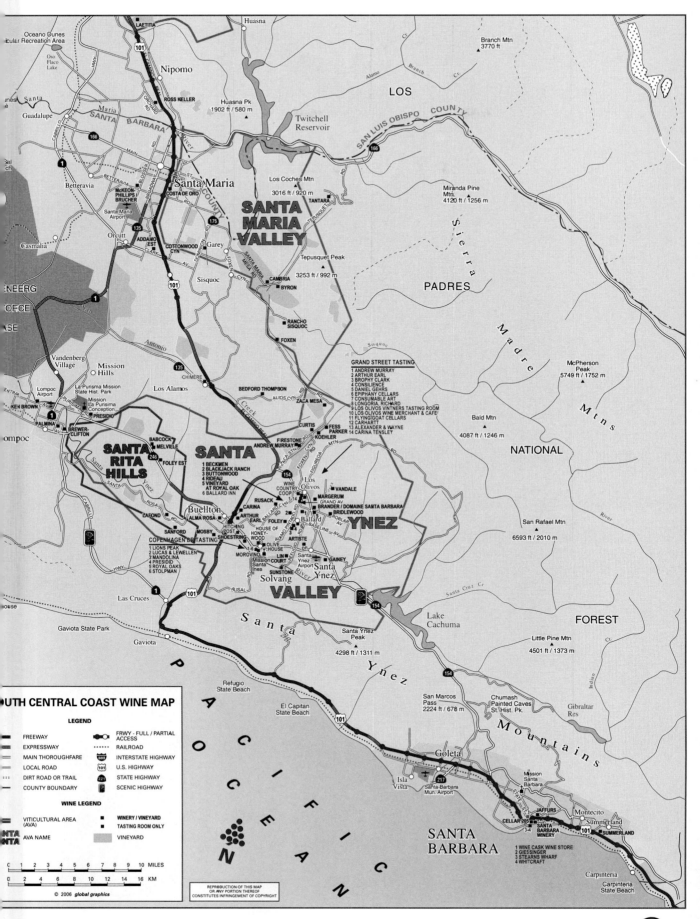

SOUTH CENTRAL COAST WINE MAP

LEGEND

- FREEWAY
- EXPRESSWAY
- MAIN THOROUGHFARE
- LOCAL ROAD
- DIRT ROAD OR TRAIL
- COUNTY BOUNDARY

- FRWY - FULL / PARTIAL ACCESS
- RAILROAD
- INTERSTATE HIGHWAY
- U.S. HIGHWAY
- STATE HIGHWAY
- SCENIC HIGHWAY

WINE LEGEND

- VITICULTURAL AREA (AVA)
- AVA NAME

- WINERY / VINEYARD
- TASTING ROOM ONLY
- VINEYARD

0 1 2 3 4 5 6 7 8 9 10 MILES
0 2 4 6 8 10 12 14 16 KM

© 2006 *global graphics*

REPRODUCTION OF THIS MAP OR ANY PORTION THEREOF CONSTITUTES INFRINGEMENT OF COPYRIGHT

Highway 1 near Guadalupe

Along Highway 154

Rancher Roza near Cayucos

Like the Napa and Sonoma Valleys, this region is located near the Pacific Ocean and is separated from this huge body of water by mountain ranges. The Central Coast, however, has an extra advantage, as the mountain ranges run east-to-west, allowing a 'wide open door' to misty fog and cool ocean breezes over the vineyards, protecting grapes from the searing heat that would otherwise devastate the harvest. So, the unimpeded fog and ocean breezes make the grapes "cooler" than other grapes which causes them to ripen more slowly, thus making for a longer growing season. Much of the land was once at the bottom of the ocean. Later, coastal rivers deposited rocky, alluvial soils which allow for excellent drainage and low nutrition.

Farm country around Santa Maria is noted for its sandy soils, particularly west of Highway 101.

Highway 154 connects Goleta (north of Santa Barbara) through the Santa Ynez Valley to Los Olivos, heart of Santa Barbara County's wine region.

WINE ACCESSORIES

Bottle types used in California are generally along the lines of those used in Europe today: Bordeaux, Burgundy or the Hochheim ("Hock") types. The latter is used for German style wines.

Bordeaux bottles are either dark green or clear. The green is used for red wines such as Merlot, Cabernet Sauvignon and Zinfandel, clear glass is for Sauvignon Blanc, Fume Blanc, White Zinfandel, etc.

Burgundy bottles are shaped somewhat like Champagne bottles on a smaller scale. The dark green glass is used for a great variety of wines, red (Pinot Noir),white, dry or sweet.

Corks are made from the inner bark of a species of oak tree grown in Spain and Portugal. There has been widespread use of plastic corks to avoid the aftertaste that cork may leave. The newest trend is towards screw caps, to avoid contamination and for easier opening.

At Mission La Purisima, the padres pressed their fruit with a wooden press. It stands today as a romantic symbol of their introduction of wine cultivation and olive growing to California. Today's vintners often use massive "crushers" to process a large tonnage of grapes.

PINOT NOIR

Burgundy

Wine glasses, or stemware, are selected to enhance the enjoyment of the wine. Some have a large, full bowl, such as burgundy glasses which can allow moderate tannins to reach the tongue directly.

Bourdeaux

Glasses with narrower bowls and a smaller circumference at the rim, like those used for bordeaux wines, may be preferred if the wine is high in acidity, thus enhancing the fruit taste while diminishing the tannin effect.

White wine

White wine is often poured into smaller glasses than for reds, and some white wine glasses have a notably small rim opening which directs the wine to the tip of the tongue. That way the fruity flavor comes through effectively.

Port/Sherry

Sweet wines such as port or sherry are often served in glasses with shorter stems than those for wine and with somewhat tighter rims. This rim form enhances the bouquet and directs the liquid to the front of the tongue - the 'sugar zone'.

Champagne/Sekt

Traditionally in the U.S., "champagne" glasses had wide, open rims, which let much of the carbonation escape, thus the "bubbly" didn't stay that way for long. German "Sekt" is served in an elogated, narrow glass to keep the bubbles working. Today's glass fashions are tending towards the narrower style.

Wine and Art seem to go together comfortably. Local artist Bob Burridge paints almost daily in his country barn studio located in Arroyo Grande. Art critics describe his 'real life style' as "vibrant, beautiful, masterly done and just a little tweaked" and "His use of bold, rich color and adventurous texture, while complex, is uplifting and Pop." His current subjects feature "the Good Life," which naturally includes wine.

Many local artists are shown in the galleries of Santa Ynez, Solvang, Cambria, San Luis Obispo and Santa Barbara.

BOB BURRIDGE   Photo: Jeff May

NOSE includes aroma of the grapes, hints of such things as bell pepper in Cabernet Sauvignon. "Nose" may also have defective smells such as acidity, or vinegary smells, sulfur dioxide which smells like a burnt match or others like rotten eggs or sauerkraut. "Nose" also can be attributed to smell of the oak barrels in which wine is aged - if it is aged just the right amount of time, there is a faint smell of vanilla, otherwise the oak smell becomes distracting.

RETRONASAL aroma is detected at the back of the nose. When wine is sipped and "chewed", thus coating the mouth, aroma seeps up to the olfactory glands, an indication of the wine's quality. The "finish" is the persistance of this olfactory experience.

BOUQUET is the complex blend of smells produced by fermentation, such as yeasty and flowery smells arising during aging. Smells are created by the grape sorts themselves, the yeast which may be added, and the wood from the barrels in which the wine is aged. Wine is often described with terms such as berry, lemon, roses, licorice, pepper, hay, mint or toast. **TASTE** can be notably sweet, sour, salty or bitter.

A wine's **BODY** refers to the fullness of the wine in your mouth, round, not flat or thin. **TANNINS** are the astringent compounds in grape skins. **LEGS** of the wine are the streaks which run down the inside of the glass when the wine is swirled, an effect of the alcohol content. **HEAT** indicates the percentage of alcohol. **FINISH** describes how long the flavors last on the tongue.

LOOK at the color and clarity of the wine, which should be free of impurities, bright and not cloudy nor dull. If wine is too old (this varies as to the type of wine, some reds can be stored for decades), oxidation darkens the wine. A young wine will show the same color as it thins along the rim. Red color which thins to a bluish or purple color may mean grapes were not very ripe when picked. If the red thins to a deep orange, the wine is well-aged and reaching its perfection. **SWIRL** the wine in the glass to open up the "nose". Put your nose into the glass to **BREATHE** the bouquet and aroma. **TASTE** the wine on your tongue. Professional wine tasters will not drink the wine, but will **SPIT** it out. What a shame! Typically, a small piece of bread or cracker will be nibbled between tasting different wines in order to clean the palette. COLOR and CLARITY should be brilliant, clear, free of tartrate crystals, which settle on the bottom of the bottle and look like salt crystals. Red wines range from ruby to garnet shades, straw-like colors are typical for chardonnays, chenin blancs, etc.

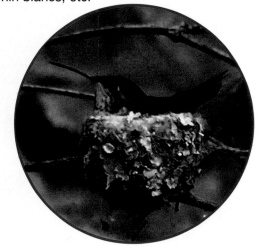

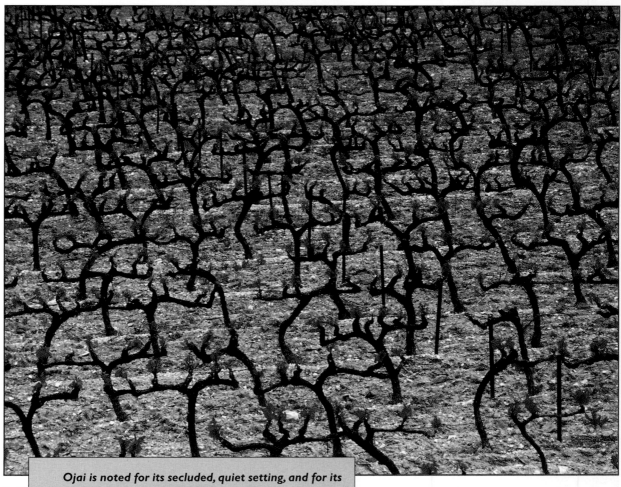

Ojai is noted for its secluded, quiet setting, and for its art galleries. The Ojai Valley Inn with its spa and golf course, draws well-healed travelers.

Ojai Valley Historical Museum displays local flora, fauna and Chumash Indian artifacts.

OJAI

CHENIN BLANC

OJAI is tucked away in a verdant valley surrounded by mountains. It was known to the Chumash Indians as "A'hwai", their word for moon. Settled as a health resort in the 1870s, it has grown to be attractive for golfers, artists, musicians, and naturalists. Ojai has its own Center for the Arts and is also noted for "The Ojai", the oldest amateur tennis event in the U.S. and for its Music Festival

Lake Casitas with 100 miles (160 km) of shoreline, is popular with locals for boating, fishing and camping.

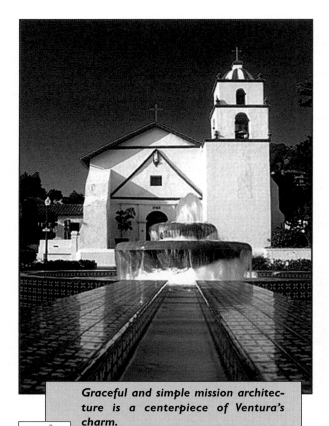

Graceful and simple mission architecture is a centerpiece of Ventura's charm.

The neoclassic style of City Hall was dominant in the early 20th Century. This building by A.C. Martin, Sr. was dedicated in 1913.

VENTURA offers uncrowded beaches, a quaint Mediterranean-style Harbor Village, the Pier & Promenade, the Ortega Adobe and Olivas Adobe historic homes. The County Museum of History and Art has a collection reflecting local history, as do the A.J. Comstock Fire Museum and the Old Livery Arts Center.

The Albinger Archaeological Museum exhibits artifacts over 3,500 years old. Channel Islands National Park Visitors Center is located at Ventura Harbor, from which full and island excursions are available.

SAN BUENAVENTURA, ninth mission in the chain, was founded on Easter Sunday in 1782 by Father Serra and dedicated to St. Bonaventure. It was the last mission the humble priest would christen. Restored in 1957, the facade exhibits an unusual triangular design which opens into the gardens. A museum exhibits artifacts that include two old wooden bells, the only ones of their type known in California. Situated three blocks from the ocean, the mission fronts on the main street of town. 225 E. Main St., Ventura.

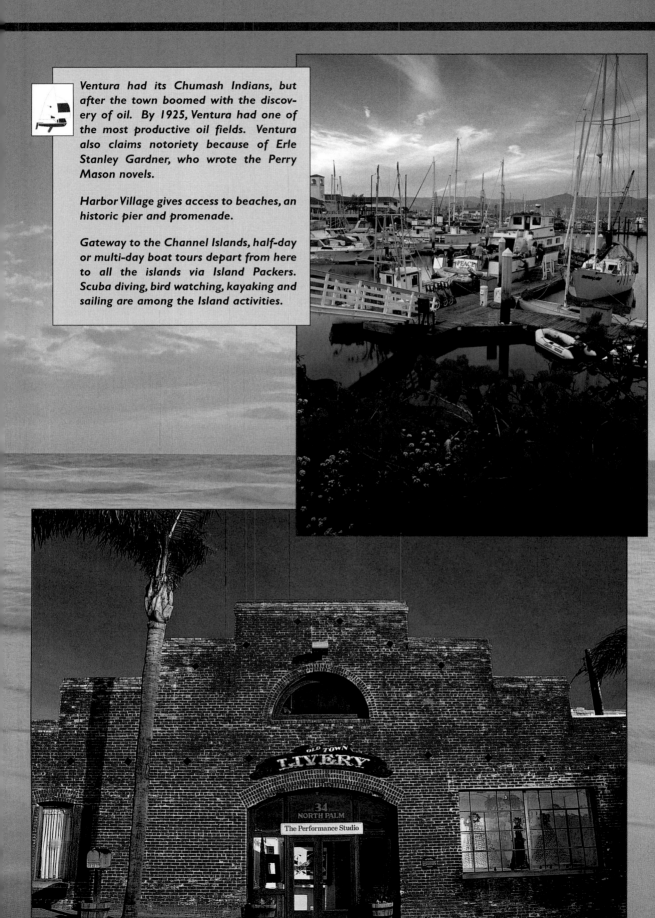

Ventura had its Chumash Indians, but after the town boomed with the discovery of oil. By 1925, Ventura had one of the most productive oil fields. Ventura also claims notoriety because of Erle Stanley Gardner, who wrote the Perry Mason novels.

Harbor Village gives access to beaches, an historic pier and promenade.

Gateway to the Channel Islands, half-day or multi-day boat tours depart from here to all the islands via Island Packers. Scuba diving, bird watching, kayaking and sailing are among the Island activities.

MONTECITO

MONTECITO has been a wealthy community since 1890s when large estates were built there. The Montecito Inn was built in 1928 by Charlie Chaplin as a getaway for Hollywood celebrities.

CARPINTERIA was named for the building activities of the Chumash Indian carpenters who found tar here which they used for their canoes. Today the area is noted for walnut groves, flower-growing and for great surfing beaches. Life during the early 20th century is depicted at the Valley Historical Museum. Orchids are grown in the Stewart Orchid greenhouses. Summerland is a great lookout point towards the Channel Islands.

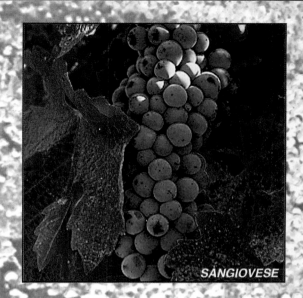

SANGIOVESE

CHARLIE CHAPLIN

RIESLING

Wild pointsettia plants grow along the highway above the vineyards of southern Santa Barbara County.

SANTA BARBARA

SANTA BARBARA, with its background of the Santa Ynez Mountains and foreground of the Pacific Ocean, is a lush plain which has attracted settlers since the late 1700s, when the Spanish soldiers came (1782) and founded a Presidio and the "Queen of the Missions", Mission Santa Barbara (built 1786, restored 1820). The Presidio is preserved in El Presidio de Santa Barbara State Historic Park, which is still undergoing excavation. One of the most attractive buildings is the Santa Barbara County Courthouse (1929) built in Spanish-Moorish style. The Courthouse is the start of a self-guided "Red Tile Tour" past many local places from the city's early history. Nearby is El Paseo, a shopping arcade built around the 1827 De la Guerra family's adobe and La Arcada with shops, galleries and restaurants. The Historical Museum features artifacts of the Spanish, Mexican and early American periods. The Museum of Art has paintings by several 20th century American artists, 19th century French Impressionists, as well as photography, prints, and drawings. It also showcases the region's many artists. Paseo Nuevo is a major shopping center with Spanish-style architecture to fit in with the city's tradition. Inland from the Wharf is the Moreton Bay Fig Tree (planted in 1877), which has become a symbol of the city. Antique shops line both sides of Brinkerhoff Avenue between Cota and Haley Streets. Nearby is the Fernald Mansion, a Victorian home and the Trussell-Winchester Adobe, partially built using materials from a shipwreck.

©Rancho San Marcos Golf Course

Palms grace the Santa Barbara Lagoon at Chase Palm Park. Day and night people stroll or bike or rollerskate on the paved areas along West Cabrillo Blvd.

The Moreton Bay Fig Tree, planted in 1877 is now a historical landmark, deeded to the City of Santa Barbara. Its branches spread 160 feet and is has been estimated that 16,000 people may find shade under its 21,000 sq. feet span.

EL PASEO

The Santa Barbara County Courthouse (1929) is typical of Mission/Spanish Colonial Revival architecture. A self-guided "Red Tile Walking Tour" covers 12 city blocks and includes the Museum of Art, Casa de la Guerra, Oreña Adobes, El Presidio and the City's Historical Museum.

From their humble, thatch-roofed beginnings to the stately adobes we see today, the missions represent a dynamic chapter of California's past. By the time the last mission was built in 1823, the Golden State had grown from an untamed wilderness to a thriving agricultural frontier on the verge of American statehood.

The 21 missions that comprise California's historic mission trail are all located on or near Highway 101, which roughly traces El Camino Real (The Royal Road) named in honor of the Spanish monarchy which financed the expeditions into California in the quest for empire. From San Diego to Los Angeles, the historic highway is now known as Interstate 5. From Santa Clarita to San Francisco, the road is called State Highway 82. North of San Francisco, Highway 101 again picks up the trail to the mission at San Rafael. From there, State Highway 37 leads to the last mission at Sonoma.

SANTA BARBARA MISSION

Founded in 1786, the "Queen of the Missions" was the first to be christened by Father Lasuen, and has continuously served as a parish church for the local population since its founding.

The church was destroyed in 1925 by an earthquake; however, restorations have returned it to its original grandeur of wrought iron, terrra cotta and carved wood. Patterned after an ancient Latin chapel in pre-Christian Rome, its twin bell towers and Doric facade present an imposing impression of strength. Located on a hilltop overlooking Santa Barbara, this mission provides a spectacular view of the ocean. The museum contains a vast store of historical material and displays many original items.

State Street is the main thoroughfare of downtown Santa Barbara. Its pleasant shops, restaurants and arcades attract visitors to the "American Riviera". North of town in Goleta is the University of Calif.-Santa Barbara.

Padres were responsible for planting vineyards and had brought cuttings with them in 1782. Their largest vineyard was along the San Jose Creek in what is now Goleta.

SANTA BARBARA HARBOR

At the heart of the city's waterfront, flanked by wide beaches, is Stearns Wharf, built in 1872 and representative of wooden wharfs of the period. It still serves the community and tourists for whale-watching, fishing, swiming and shopping. At the Wharf's Sea Center, an aquarium, 'touch tank' and a replica of a California gray whale attract young and old. Also on the Wharf is the Nature Conservancy Visitors Center which displays information about its various projects. The beach area is active with volleyball games, roller skaters, parasailing, wind surfing and an Arts & Crafts show which takes place on Sundays and holidays from 10 a.m. to dusk. Between the East Beach and Highway 101 are the Zoo and Andrée Clark Bird Refuge, centered on a lagoon with many species including waterfowl. Twenty miles offshore, the Channel Islands National Park consists of five offshore islands with their own unique plants and animals, a sanctuary of sea creatures and waterfowl. The islands are also great for diving, sea-kayaking, camping and hiking. Channel Islands Marine Sanctuary day-tours depart from Sea Landing, in particular visiting Santa Cruz Island.

The Natural History Museum displays local flora and fauna and artifacts from Chumash Indian culture. The Carriage and Western Arts Museum houses all kinds of vehicles from pioneering Santa Barbara families. Karpeles Manuscript Library Museum has a significant collection of old works of famous musicians and writers. Brooks Institute of Photography has three campuses in the area, all of which have photographic galleries. Santa Barbara Botanic Gardens, nestled in the foothills of the Santa Ynez Mountains, is 65 acres (27 hectares) of native cacti, wildflowers, redwood trees and Southern California shrubs.

Stearn's Wharf is the heart of Santa Barbara's harbor and is home to the Sea Center Maritime Museum.
Across the Shoreline Drive is the Santa Barbara Visitors Center.

Ventura Sunset

BUELLTON

BUELLTON is a good refueling point along the highway. In 1924, Split Pea Anderson's Restaurant was established, and still serves those traveling to the nearby wineries, lakes and llama or ostrich ranches. Lake Cachuma, a man-made lake and source of Santa Barbara's water is a good place to observe bald eagles.

South of Lake Cachuma off Highway 154 is Chumash Painted Cave State Historic Park

MOSBY

which preserves prehistoric paintings by the original inhabitants of the area. East of Buellton on State Highway 154 is the charming Los Olivos, once a stage-coach stop. Mattei's Tavern, still in operation today, began in 1886 as a hotel restaurant serving the coaches.

A.J.SPURS SALOON

Chumash Indians lived in the area from Paso Robles down to Malibu and inland to the San Joaquin Valley. They built domed huts made of willow and were hunters, fishermen and made their boats from redwood or driftwood found in the Pacific Ocean, sealing them with local tar.

Andersen's Pea Soup Restaurant has been established since 1924 and they have been serving simple fare to the many people traveling up Highway 101 ever since.

More recently the Chumash Indian Tribe has built its Chumash Casino/Resort inland from Solvang/Buellton, to attract visitors from all over Southern California.

Several restaurants became noteworthy from scenes in the 2004 movie "Sideways", bringing tourists an awareness of things to see and do in the Santa Ynez Valley.

Mosby Winery tasting room is located in an old carriage house, typical of early Santa Barbara pioneering life.

Ostrich Land on Highway 246 in Buellton welcomes visitors to pet their curious critters. The animals are raised here for their fine meat.

SOLVANG - windmills, bakeries, horse-drawn "honen" streetcars, 19th century timber structures place visitors to the "Danish Capital of America" out of California's usual context. The Hans Christian Andersen Museum memorializes the 'father of the modern fairy tale'. At the Elverhoj Museum, Solvang's historical heritage is preserved. The Western Wear Museum is open by reservation only to those wanting to see western gear from cowboy stars of the "Silver Screen".

Nearby is the Old Mission Santa Ines, started in 1804, almost totally destroyed in 1812 by an earthquake, burnt in a Chumash Indian revolt in 1824, in ruins by 1884 and since restored. Outdoor theatrical performances take place at the Festival Theatre. There are many opportunities to play golf throughout the Valley, or to gamble at the Chumash Casino.

The Vintage Motorcycle Museum features vehicles from the private collection of Virgil Elings. It is a broad selection with something for everyone, ranging from a 1910 FN to the present, and across all makes. The emphasis is on racing motorcycles as Virgil and his son Jeff were involved in vintage motorcycle racing, both motocross and road racing.

As an effort to preserve local culture, Solvang has its Elverhøj Museum, which features displays dedicated to the town's history, its artists and to the Danish-American pioneers who established the town in 1910.

In recent years, more and more local wineries have opened their tasting rooms in town for the convenience of the many visitors. Several are found along Mission Drive and on Copenhagen Drive.

Classic Northern European architecture is typical of many of Solvangs buildings, for example at the Wine Country Inn.

Windmills are typical of the Solvang street scene. Every Wednesday there is a Farmers Market downtown. Even "Honen" carriages draw by Belgian draft horses add to Solvang's homey atmosphere.

SANTA YNEZ was the center of the Valley's activities in the late 1800s. Santa Ynez Valley Historical Museum displays artifacts from early settlers, ranchers, farmers and from Chumash Indians. Next to it is the Parks-Janeway Carriage House, an extensive collection of horse-drawn vehicles and a notable saddle collection. Nearby are wineries and the Santa Ynez Airport for glider rides over the hills and vineyards. The Chumash Casino features card and video gaming. Los Olivos has many art galleries in its old Victorian-era buildings.

On Mission and Copenhagen Drives are tasting rooms of many local wineries. There are almost 100 wineries in Santa Barbara County. Here an appropriate whimisical carving adorns the entrance to Lucas & Lewellen.

A lush waterfall cascades down 80 feet in Nojoqui Falls County Park just outside of Solvang along Alisal Road. It is a 15 minute hike off the road to the Falls.

MISSION SANTA INÉS

Named for a 13 year-old Roman martyr, St. Agnes, who refused to sacrifice to the pagan gods in 304 AD, Mission Santa Ines was dedicated in 1804 by Father Estevan Tapis. Amazingly, it survived the numerous earthquakes. The museum contains a notable collection of vestments, church records and missals, and the church displays some of the original decorations on a wall behind the alter. A historic grape arbor shelters a walkway that transports the visitor back in time, emerging in the lovely gardens that appear today much as they did nearly 200 years ago. 1760 Mission Dr., Solvang

The surrounding town takes its anglicized name "Santa Ynez" from Ines, Spanish for Agnes.

From the Mission gorunds one has a panoramic view of part of the Santa Ynez Valley and of the San Rafael mountains.

This is the "hidden gem" of the 21 Missions throughout California.

Santa Ines Mission is very much an active parish as well as an essential part of community life. Besides religious services, community groups use the facilities for annual events such as the Story Telling Festival and the Rancheros Visadores Horse-Riding event.

The grounds are used as a staging area for local parades and biking events.

Quicksilver Miniature Horse Ranch, on the road from Solvang to Los Olivos, is home to award-winning miniatures since 1983. At any time, there are 25-30 foals being bred here. Gentle, patient creatures, they are smaller than some large dogs and make excellent pets. When hitched to a wagon, they can pull up to 10 times their weight.

RURAL SETTINGS

LA FOND

Breathe in fresh ocean air wafting over the Santa Rita Hills and along Highway 246. Stop for a gaze at the many flower fields in the region. Marigolds are grown here for their seed and for food coloring.

WINERIES AT WORK

Field workers start in the early morning hours to hand cut the grape clusters. The cooler morning temperatures helps with the retention of juice. The buckets are emptied into large bins which are then dumped into tanks. From there the grapes go on their way to crushing, fermenting, barrel-aging and bottling.

Workers are continually in motion, moving the grapes along the processing 'trail'. It is a hot, dusty job and has to be done within a short period of time, while the grapes are at their juiciest.

In the larger wineries, vats of grape juice are siphoned into American or French Oak barrels for aging.

BRIDLEWOOD

Originally known locally as an equestrian rehabilitation facility, in 1998 Bridlewood Estate was made into a winery, maintaining its Mission-style architecture.

SANTA YNEZ

Harvest is a time of uncertainty and dealing with the unknown, whether it is equipment malfunction or heat spikes in the weather that turns the process into a frantic race to get the grapes off the vines.

When to pick is a winemaker's responsibility. Judging at what point the grapes will produce the most flavorful and balanced wine is critical. Winemakers walk the vineyards sampling the fruit and relying on their sensory instincts and lab analyses to determine ripeness. Theyneed to be practical about the logistical constraints of harvest - to how many tons of grapes can be picked in a day, how many tanks are available and how much their cellar crew can handle. A winemaker's depth of knowledge regarding the vineyards that produce the fruit is perhaps the most important aspect of the job. Whether working for a large winery that contracts with multiple growers or on a small vineyard estate, the winemaker needs to have enough experience and awareness to make decisions about the ripeness, flavors, acidity and condition of the grapes. Each vintage is different, and winemakers need to use their training and intuitive skills to work with every season.

California winemakers have usually completed a four-year Bachelor of Science degree in viticulture and enology with courses in viticulture, pests and diseases, plant physiology, enology, microbiology, fining and others. A handful receive a Masters in viticulture and enology each year. Winemakers love the challenge of harvest, the time of year when their knowledge and actions impact an entire vintage of wine. They usually work seven days a week for two to three months, as they need to be in constant communication with their growers and cellar staff.

WINEMAKER D. HOPKINS

The winemaker studies:

Vi•ti•cul•ture - n. : the cultivation or culture of grapes, especially for wine making.

Vi•ni•fi•ca•tion - n.: the conversion of fruit juices (as grape juice) into wine by fermentation.

Enol•o•gy (brit.: Oenol•o•gy) - n.: a science that deals with wine and wine making.

ARCHITECTURE and AMBIENCE

Winemakers are also responsible for budgets, purchasing winemaking equipment, managing inventory, and many other managerial responsibilities depending on the size of the winery. Many winemakers spend time traveling to different cities, meeting with media and trade to help promote and market their wines. These 'Renaissance' men and women are leaders and innovators in the California wine industry. They often take inspiration for their own premises from European "Mediterranean - style" architecture.

SUNSTONE

SUNSTONE

Recreating an ambience with European notes, but with distinctly Californian flavor, some wineries select the Bodega style, others a French Chateau, still others the romance of an Italian villa.

SANTA YNEZ

A grapevine planted in 1842 on a farm in Carpinteria grew to monstrous proportions. In fifty years, it had a trunk measuring nine feet around, an arbor covering two acres and an annual yield of ten tons of grapes!

The wine industry has enjoyed a renaissance in Santa Barbara County in the last 25 years. Early studies by researchers from U.C. Davis found that Santa Barbara County was cooler than most wine regions of Northern California and that it had an excellent balance of geology, climate, soil and water. This gave it great potential as a viticultural area. The first modern vineyards were planted in the Tepusquet area of the Santa Maria Valley in the early 1960s. Shortly after that, vineyards were planted in several parts of the Santa Ynez Valley.

Currently there are more than 100 wineries in Santa Barbara County located primarily in the Santa Ynez Valley, Santa Rita Hills and Santa Maria Valley appellations. Most of the wineries are small businesses, run by individuals or families. The wine industry in Santa Barbara County grew from virtually nothing in 1970 to a $360 million business more than 30 years later. Over a million cases of wine are produced annually. Today there are over 21,000 acres of vineyards in Santa Barbara County. At more than $160,365,223, wine grapes are, after strawberries, the most valuable crop in the County.

Santa Barbara County has a history of winemaking and winegrape growing stretching back more than 200 years to before California was a state. From the Mission Era of early California through the Ranchero and Pueblo Era, vintners stuggled through Prohibition to the beginning of the modern era of viniculuture that started in the 60's. Santa Barbara County continues to combine traditional, hand-made techniques, with the latest cutting-edge innovations in grape-growing and winemaking.

Father Junipero Serra brought grapevine cuttings from Mexico in 1782 to be planted in the fertile bottoms of Sycamore Creek (in what is now known as the Milpas district of Santa Barbara). The largest mission vineyard, about 25 acres, was located in the San Jose Creek area, and an adobe winery, built nearby in 1804, is now Goleta's oldest landmark. In 1884, Justinian Caire imported grape slips from France and planted a 150-acre vineyard on Santa Cruz Island. His prize-winning wines were shipped to San Francisco for bottling.

Stagecoach, horse and buggy, wagons, and horseback were the only means of transportation from Los Angeles to the small towns of the Central Coast until the opening of the Pacific Coast Railway in the early 1880's.
Oil was discovered at the turn of the 20th century in the region, which also brought many settlers, some of them Europeans who brought with them their passion for wine.

The wines of this region have earned great respect among knowledgeable wine drinkers and have won an impressive array of medals in regional, national and international competitions. The wines frequently receive overall sweepstakes, double golds and platinums, and best-of-class awards, as well as excellent reviews. Santa Barbara County is well-known for fine Chardonnay, Pinot Noir and Syrah, as well as Sauvignon Blanc, Cabernet Sauvignon, Riesling and other varietals.

The annual Spring Santa Barbara County Vintners' Festivals attracts wine lovers from near and far for an opportunity to meet vintners from many wineries, and to taste their wines. The Celebration of Harvest festival is held in October during the excitement of the wine grape harvest. As well as the Festivals themselves, these weekends are filled with open houses, winemaker dinners, special tastings and other unique events.

ARTISTE GALLERY

OLD STAGE COACH STOP

PASTORAL LIVING

OLD GAS STATION

The Santa Ynez Valley Museum and Parks-Janeway Carriage House has one of the most extensive collections of American made carriages in the West.

RIDEAU

RURAL ACCOMODATIONS

Many people remember actor Fess Parjer for his portrayal of frontiersmen Davy Crockett and Daniel Boone on TV in the late 1950's and 60's. Blending his gracious Texas hospitality and tremendous eye for real estate development, Parker built an ocean front resort in 1986, "Fess Parker's Double Tree Resort" in Santa Barbara.

In 1987, Parker purchased a 714 acre ranch in the Santa Ynez Valley, where he established Fess Parker's Winery & Vineyard. The Parker family has re-ceived numerous awards for producing some of the region's finest wines.

The folling year Parker purchased The Grand Hotel in Los Olivos, a charming 21 room Victorian-style inn now named the "Fess Parker's Wine Country Inn & Spa". Visiting guests may have the opportunity to see the legend himself, as he frequently dines in the restaurant.

FESS PARKER INN

Firestone Vineyard was Santa Barbara County's first estate winery (1972), and is a cornerstone of coastal estate winemaking. The business spans three generations of the Firestone family and eight includes eight individual vineyards in the Santa Ynez Valley.

grapes. Firestone Vineyard's estate soils range from sand to gravelly loam with rocky subsoils, thus these well-draining soils are optimal for wine-growing, forcing vine roots deep into ground and ultimately generating more concentrated varietal flavors.

Viticulture in Santa Barbara County's Santa Ynez Valley benefits from the unique east-to-west orientation of the sur-rounding mountain ranges which are open to the Pacific Ocean at their western extreme. A cool-ing maritime influence extends the growing sea-son and encourages the development of exquisite-ly balanced and flavorful

BLACKJACK

FIRESTONE

LOS OLIVOS TASTING ROOMS

Los Olivos was founded in 1861 when the Overland-Coast Line Stage line ran from San Francisco through Los Olivos to Los Angeles and on to San Diego.

Wilding Art Museum in the old Keenan-Hartley House features exhibitions on the theme of America's wilderness and offers a number of lectures, classes, workshops, films, trips, and other activities relating to art and nature.

Los Olivos Cafe
& Wine Merchant

WINE TASTING

1886

MATTEI'S TAVERN

Los Olivos is virtually the cross-roads of Santa Barbara's wine country. Mattei's Tavern had been the final hotel and restaurant stop for railway and coach passengers since 1886.

Charming Los Olivos Cafe & Wine Merchant (at left) is at the heart of Los Olivos culinary activities. It was featured in the movie "Sideways".

CABERNET SAUVIGNON

Along Highway 166

Figueroa Mountain

Foxen Canyon Road

SANTA MARIA

Areas that have been designated official wine growing regions by the ATF (Federal Bureau of Alcohol, Tobacco and Firearms) are called American Viticultural Areas (AVAs). In Europe they are referred to as Appellations.

An AVA designation requires that 85% of the wine must come from the AVA, which are geographic locations that have the same climate, soil, elevations and other specific characteristics.

An AVA is considered a type of appellation and both are often used interchangeably, although appellations are often not used by the ATF.

There can be sub-AVAs thus smaller areas located within the region that has an AVA, have their own AVAs. An AVA based on geographic regions tells you what varietals are suited for growing in that specific AVA. If a wine comes from any particular AVA, that is not a reflection on its quality - good or bad.

ZINFANDEL

"Estated Bottled" wines means it must meet the requirements of the ATF, which is that the wine must come from grapes grown entirely on the premises of the winery. The wine must be made and bottled at the winery.

"Reserve Wines" have no legal meaning in the U.S., but often the winery will use the term Reserve for the bottling of a special wine which may be of higher quality and/or of limited production. Often the term is used for marketing purposes and does not necessarily reflect anything about the wine's quality.

JOHN KRSKA

 A winemaker's relationship with growers or vineyard managers is usually one of close cooperation and communication. Many are long-term relationships built on trust and a shared vision of how to achieve certain parameters for making the finest wine possible from a given vineyard site.

57

SANTA MARIA - PISMO BEACH

TWITCHELL RESERVOIR

LOS COCHES PASS

PISMO BEACH

PISMO BEACH besides being "Clam Capital of the World", is a resort area comprised of Avila Beach, Grover Beach and Oceano. At Pismo State Beach, ATVs (all-terrain vehicles) can be rented to ride the Oceano Dunes State Vehicular Recreation Area (entrances at Grover Beach and Oceano). Other sports include horseback riding, surfing, and body-boarding. Outlet shopping is at Pismo Beach Outlet Center.

Mineral spas are found near Avila Beach, and inland are the Edna Valley/Arroyo Grande Valley areas, housing 15 wineries nestled below the Santa Lucia Mountains. Arroyo Grande, founded in 1862, is interesting for its restored 1890s buildings at the Arroyo Grande Village, and for a suspension footbridge. The town holds an annual Strawberry Festival on Memorial Day weekend. Nipomo is another agricultural town known for citrus orchards, vegetables and flower nurseries.

PISMO BEACH

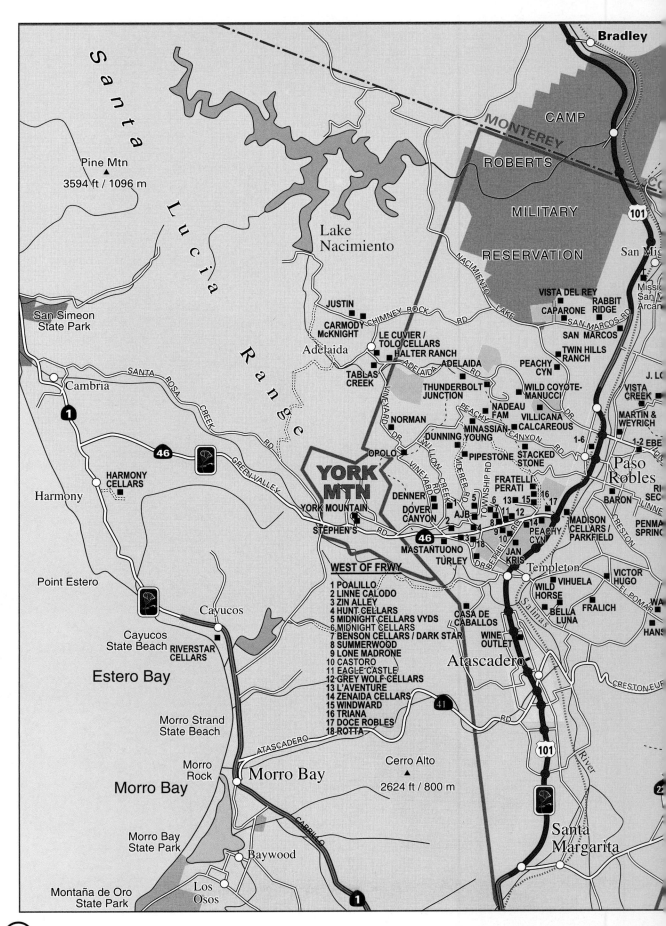

Bradley

CAMP
ROBERTS
MILITARY
RESERVATION

MONTEREY

101

San Mig

Pine Mtn
3594 ft / 1096 m

Santa Lucia Range

Lake
Nacimiento

NACIMIENTO LAKE

San Simeon
State Park

VISTA DEL REY
CAPARONE   RABBIT
RIDGE

Missi
San M
Arcar

SAN MARCOS RD

JUSTIN

CHIMNEY ROCK   RD

SAN MARCOS

CARMODY
McKNIGHT

Adelaida

SANTA

ROSA

Cambria

CREEK

RD

LE CUVIER /
TOLO CELLARS
HALTER RANCH
ADELAIDA

TWIN HILLS
RANCH

ADELAIDA
RD

PEACHY
CYN

J. LO

TABLAS
CREEK

VINEYARD

THUNDERBOLT
JUNCTION

WILD COYOTE-
MANUCCI

VISTA
CREEK

PEACHY

NORMAN

DR

NADEAU
FAM

VILLICANA

CANYON

MARTIN &
WEYRICH

MINASSIAN CALCAREOUS
DUNNING YOUNG

RD

1-6

1-2 EBE

OPOLO

WILLOW

CREEK

RD

PIPESTONE   STACKED
STONE

Paso
Robles

46

HARMONY
CELLARS

GREEN VALLEY

RD

YORK
MTN

VINEYARD

RD

FRATELLI
PERATI

16

17

RI
SEC

Harmony

DENNER

5

6   13   15

BARON

LINNE

PENMA
SPRING

YORK MOUNTAIN

DOVER
CANYON

7   11   12

1

14

Point Estero

STEPHEN'S

RD

46

AJB

2

9

10

PEACHY
CYN

MADISON
CELLARS /
PARKFIELD

MASTANTUONO
TURLEY

3   18

JAN
KRIS

Templeton

VICTOR
HUGO

Cayucos

Cayucos
State Beach   RIVERSTAR
CELLARS

WEST OF FRWY
1 POALILLO
2 LINNE CALODO
3 ZIN ALLEY
4 HUNT CELLARS
5 MIDNIGHT CELLARS VYDS
6 MIDNIGHT CELLARS
7 BENSON CELLARS / DARK STAR
8 SUMMERWOOD
9 LONE MADRONE
10 CASTORO
11 EAGLE CASTLE
12 GREY WOLF CELLARS
13 L'AVENTURE
14 ZENAIDA CELLARS
15 WINDWARD
16 TRIANA
17 DOCE ROBLES
18 ROTTA

CASA DE
CABALLOS

WINE
OUTLET

Atascadero

VIHUELA

WILD
HORSE

BELLA
LUNA

FRALICH

EL POMAR

WA

HANS

Estero Bay

Salinas

CRESTON

Morro Strand
State Beach

ATASCADERO

41

Cerro Alto
2624 ft / 800 m

CRESTON EUF

RD

101

River

Morro
Rock

Morro Bay

Morro Bay

CARRILLO

Morro Bay
State Park

Baywood

Santa
Margarita

Montaña de Oro
State Park

Los
Osos

1

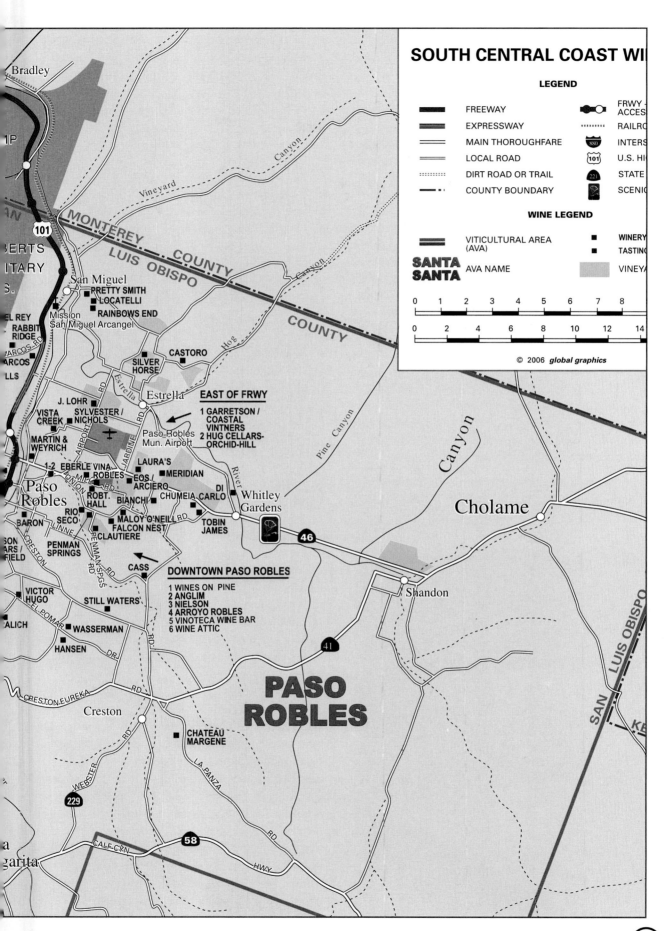

SOUTH CENTRAL COAST WI...

LEGEND

━━━	FREEWAY		⬤━⬤	FRWY ACCES...
═══	EXPRESSWAY		··········	RAILRO...
───	MAIN THOROUGHFARE		🛡880	INTERS...
───	LOCAL ROAD		101	U.S. HI...
··········	DIRT ROAD OR TRAIL		221	STATE...
─ ·· ─	COUNTY BOUNDARY		🛡	SCENIC...

WINE LEGEND

═══	VITICULTURAL AREA (AVA)		■	WINERY
SANTA SANTA	AVA NAME		■	TASTING...
				VINEYA...

0 1 2 3 4 5 6 7 8

0 2 4 6 8 10 12 14

© 2006 *global graphics*

Bradley

MONTEREY COUNTY
LUIS OBISPO COUNTY
101

San Miguel
PRETTY SMITH
LOCATELLI
RAINBOWS END
Mission
San Miguel Arcangel

Vineyard

Canyon

CASTORO
SILVER HORSE
Hog
Estrella

Estrella

EAST OF FRWY
1 GARRETSON / COASTAL VINTNERS
2 HUG CELLARS-ORCHID-HILL

J. LOHR
VISTA CREEK
SYLVESTER / NICHOLS
Paso Robles Mun. Airport

Pine Canyon

Canyon

MARTIN & WEYRICH
LAURA'S
1-2 EBERLE VINA ROBLES
EOS / ARCIERO
MERIDIAN
DI CARLO

Paso Robles

ROBT. HALL
BIANCHI
CHUMEIA

Whitley Gardens

Cholame

RIO SECO
BARON
MALOY O'NEILL
FALCON NEST
CLAUTIERE
TOBIN JAMES

46

LINNE
PENMAN SPRINGS

CASS

DOWNTOWN PASO ROBLES
1 WINES ON PINE
2 ANGLIM
3 NIELSON
4 ARROYO ROBLES
5 VINOTECA WINE BAR
6 WINE ATTIC

Shandon

VICTOR HUGO
STILL WATERS

KALICH
WASSERMAN
HANSEN

41

CRESTON-EUREKA

Creston

PASO ROBLES

CHATEAU MARGENE

WEBSTER
LA PANZA

229

CALF-CYN
58
HWY

SAN LUIS OBISPO
SAN
KE...

VANDENBERG AFB

VANDENBERG AIR FORCE BASE, known for decades as the launching site for the 30th Space Wing Command's ICBM missiles, the historic Flying Tigers and for NASA. It is also home to the California Space Port, the first commercial space launch operating facility. The base covers 99,000 acres and has approximately 3,000 buildings to support to more than 18,000 people.

The **Guadalupe-Nipomo Dunes Complex** is a National Natural Landmark comprising 18 miles and more than 22,000 acres of one of the largest coastal dune ecosystems on earth. It has achieved National Seashore status. The location of the Dunes Complex in a transition zone between northern and southern California plant and animal communities results in a high degree of habitat diversity, a large number of native plants and animals, and susceptibility to disturbing delicate ecosystem balances. With more than 1,000 known species of birds, plants and animals and some of the highest dunes on the West Coast, it is a place of rare beauty and significance.

BABCOCK

THE DUNES CENTER

The dunes complex is one of the last remaining intact coastal dunes systems in the United States, and encompasses creeks, rivers and lakes along with seemingly endless vistas of magnificent rolling dunes. Mountain lions, black bears, bobcats, and coyotes roam the constantly shifting landscape, and over 1,000 plants, animals, and insects call these sand dunes home.

The Dunes Center is located in a stunningly restored 1910 Craftsman Bungalow which has been accurately restored and provides an idea of what life was in Guadalupe at the beginning of the 20th century. One can view exhibits of Guadalupe's past, see remnants from Cecil B. DeMille's "Ten Commandments" (which was filmed in the Guadalupe Dunes Complex), as was "Pirates of the Caribbean" and "Hidalgo". There is also information on the local flora and fauna, and viewing of various films spotlighting how the dunes were formed, as well as the many people who have encountered the dunes throughout the ages.

As in many rural communities throughout the country, Santa Maria has its Elks Rodeo, held annually in early summer for over 60 years.

crops. It is known for its flower seed and cut flower production. In June, Lompoc has its annual Flower Festival. Since 1988, it is known as the "City of Murals" with over 40 painted murals in the Old Town section.

The Cypress Gallery and the Lompoc Museum, located in the historic 1910 Carnegie Library, features Chumash Indian artifacts and other local archaeological finds.

LOMPOC ("Lom-poke") was originally settled by the Chumash Indians as the heart of their society. Since its founding in 1888, Lompoc has a cozy, small town atmosphere, balmy ocean breezes, and a rich cultural history.

Lompoc Valley has rich agricultural land, producing a wide variety of

MISSION LA PURISIMA

LA PURISIMA CONCEPCION, the 11th mission, was founded in 1787 by Father Lasuen and is located 50 miles west of Santa Barbara. Considered to be the best example of mission architecture, it has 37 rooms that have been completely restored and furnished. Volunteers perform living history demonstrations of mission life such as candle making and weaving. In the garden area, water flows through a series of pools and a fountain before passing through the lavandareas where the mission women washed clothes. Plants were brought from the 20 other mission gardens to form one of the finest collections of early California flora in existence. Horses, cattle, burros and the four-horned Churro sheep graze in the quiet pastures.

LOS ALAMOS

Built in 1880, the Union Hotel below has hosted travelers by stagecoach, then by rail, and early motorists on Highway 101. Movie stars stopped to tank up at the gas station and filled up their flasks at the bar.

In the early 1950s, country music stars Johnny Cash or Buck Owens variously played the Saloon.

Today's Hotel and Mansion host special events, weddings, Civil War "Balls" and has been the site of movie and photo shoots.

South San Luis Obispo County has earned worldwide recognition and respect for the exceptional quality of wine grapes produced in this ideal viticultural area, including Edna Valley, the Arroyo Grande Valley, each a designated American Viticultural Area, the Avila Valley and Nipomo. Wine grapes are the leading crop in San Luis Obispo County, with over 3000 acres of vines in the south of the County.

The South Central Coast valleys have east-west orientations and are distinguished by the extensive maritime influence on the climate and soil. The soils are dominated by marine deposits left

APPLE FARM INN

millions of years ago when the valleys were under water. Loam and clay topsoil overlay calcareous marine deposits promoting complex flavors. Tempered marine air flows directly into the Valley from the Pacific Ocean and creates an unusually long growing season resulting in greatly intensified varietal flavors. All of these elements produce wine grapes and wines of complex flavors and intensity found only in the world's greatest wine regions.

Few wine aficionados visiting wineries in San Luis Obispo County's countryside realize that this region's wine heritage goes back about 250 years when the first grapevines were planted by Franciscan padres to make wine for sacramental purposes. It is recorded that the wines produced at the San Luis Obispo Mission earned the padres higher revenues than any other mission producing wine in California.

LAETITIA

EDNA VALLEY WINE TRAIL

Nearly 100 years later, early settlers began producing wine commercially, but it is only since the 1990s that San Luis Obispo's wine industry has really flourished, reportedly increasing 72% in the last ten years.

Today there seems no limit to the number of new vineyards being planted in the County. Vintners strive to produce ultra-premium wines from varietals best suited for this region's microclimates, earning the Valley's wine grape growers a reputation for growing superior Chardonnays. And viticulturists have proven that the soils of the Edna Valley and Arroyo Grande Valley are also ideally suited for growing Pinot Noir, Syrah, Grenache, and white Rhone varieties such as Roussanne and Viognier. Although the Edna Valley, Arroyo Grande Valley and Paso Robles appellations developed independently, all within San Luis Obispo County, there were many time parallels as the early pioneers built the foundation for today's wine industry.
In 1879 the first vineyard in Arroyo Grande was planted, but it was 1882 before the Paso Robles region had its first commercial winery established by A. York, thus

York Mountain Winery is the oldest continuiously operating winery in the County.

The Edna Valley and Arroyo Grande Valley regions did not get started commercially until 1968. By 1973-74 Chamisal Vineyard and Paragon Vineyard were planted. At Ditmas Ranch in 1974, the roots of the century-old Zinfandel vines first planted there were still alive when the Greenoughs bought the estate now known as Saucelito Canyon Winery.

Older wineries, such as Edna Valley Vineyard, have been an institution of learning for many talented local winemakers. The influx of new, small one-man operations and large wineries continues to rise. Numerous wineries outside the region have purchased grapes here for many years and are planting more vineyards. Still, the acclaim goes to this region's early pioneering vintners who proved the reputation of the Edna and Arroyo Grande Valleys by producing the finest wines possible.

COASTAL BEAUTY

Montaña de Oro St. Park

COASTAL BEAUTY

COASTAL BEAUTY

Guadalupe-Nipomo Dunes

MISSION
SAN LUIS OBISPO

SAN LUIS OBISPO, the settlement, was founded in 1772 as Mission San Luis Obispo de Tolosa. Nine unerupted volcanic plugs form the "peaks" along the city towards the Pacific Ocean. The streets of SLO are lined with Victorian homes, outdoor cafes and boutiques. The Jack House, an 1870s Victorian home is open as a museum. The Apple Farm Mill House still functions as a working grist mill. A Farmer's Market takes place every Thursday evening. SLO is also home to Calif. Polytechnic State University, one of 21 State campuses. The San Luis Obispo County Historical Museum exhibits artifacts of Chumash and Salinan Indians and from the area's Rancho days.

The humble chapel, Mission San Luis Obispo, built of logs, was dedicated to St. Louis, Bishop of Tolosa in 1772, and was the first mission to use tiles extensively on the roof due to repeated attacks by Indians who used flaming arrows to ignite the original thatched roof. Situated in the fertile, well-watered Valley of the Bears, the mission produced an abundance of crops, and two -powered grist mills processed foods normally ground by hand. The mission underwent an extensive restoration program in the 1930's and today welcomes visitors to its nearly-original condition.

The museum features a rare collection of early California photographs, authentic Serra relics and specimens of Chumash Indian craftsmanship.

782 Monterey St., San Luis Obispo.

MADONNA INN

The padres planted anywhere from 1,000 to 1,200 vines, but their wines were low in tannic acid and could not be aged properly because of the lack of the proper white oak barrels," according to local historian, Dan Krieger, Ph.D. Cal Poly. " The padres used the grapes to make Brandy because it had greater value and it could be shipped successfully."

Besides being home to Calif. Polytechnic State University, San Luis Obispo is known for its Film Festival in early March, Mozart Festival in early June and Shakespeare Festival mid-July.

BAILEYANA

MORRO BAY

MORRO BAY is dominated by Morro Rock, an ancient monolithic volanic outcropping in the Bay (576 ft/176 m). It was first sighted by Juan Rodriguez Cabrillo in 1542 and named "El Moro" for its dome shape. Since the late 1800's, quarrying had taken place on the sides of Morro Rock to provide material for breakwaters such as the one at Port San Luis Obispo. Morro Bay State Park has a rookery for great blue herons, and is a major stop for over 70 species of migratory birds on their way between Mexico and Northern California. There is also a Museum of Natural History in the Park. Moñtana de Oro State Park is situated on 8,000 acres (3,238 hectares) of rugged wilderness and is a favorite for hikers, mountain-bikers and for surfers along its coastal borders.

 Morro Bay Harbor Festival is held in early October, celebrating the town's importance as home of one of the State's largest commercial fishing fleets.

Paso Robles is home to more than 150 wineries and 26,000 vineyard acres focusing on premium wine production. Distinct micro-climates and diverse soils, combined with warm days and cool nights, make growing conditions ideal for producing more than 40 wine varieties from Cabernet Sauvignon and Merlot, to Syrah, Viognier and Roussanne, to Zinfandel.

In 1797 the first wine grapes were introduced to Paso Robles by the Franciscan missionaries at Mission San Miguel Arcangel. In the 1840s those vineyards were abandoned until European immigrants arrived in the 1860s. A Frenchman, Pierre Dallidet, purchased the mission's suffering vines and Englishman Henry Ditmas started the area's first vineyard importing Zinfandel and Muscat grapes from France and Spain for his 560 acre Rancho Saucelito.

The York family planted some of the area's earliest Zinfandel vines, selling their wines mostly in San Luis Obispo and eventually as far away as San Francisco. Immigrant farming families settled in the area. In 1890, Frenchman Adolf Siot planted Zinfandel west of Templeton. In the 1920's, Italian families' vineyards included Dusi, Martinelli, Vosti and Bianchi – many of which are still being farmed today by their families.

The Paso Robles wine region gained more notoriety when Ignace Paderewski, the famous

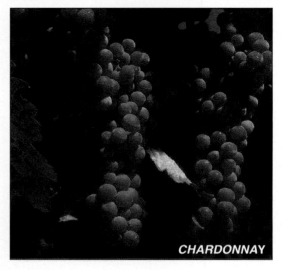
CHARDONNAY

Polish statesman and concert pianist, visited Paso Robles, became enchanted with the area, and purchased 2,000 acres. In the early 1920s, he planted Petite Sirah and Zinfandel on his Rancho San Ignacio vineyard in the Adelaida area. Of any variety, Zinfandel had a strong influence on the early growth and development of the wine industry in Paso Robles and remains a key wine varietal for several wineries, including, among others, Peachy Canyon Winery, Turley Wine Cellars, Tobin James Cellars, Norman Vineyards, Castoro Cellars and Nadeau Family Vintners.

The late 1960s and early 1970s saw a new generation of vineyardists as Dr. Stanley Hoffman, under the guidance of U.C. Davis and legendary enologist Andre Tchelistcheff, planted some of the region's first Cabernet Sauvignon, Pinot Noir and Chardonnay on his 1,200-acre ranch. His Hoffman Mountain Ranch Winery was the first large-scale modern facility in the area and one that created a stir in international wine circles in the 1970s with his Pinot Noir and Cabernet Sauvignon. Cabernet Sauvignon remains the leading varietal for the Paso Robles appellation, accounting for 30 percent of the region's planted wine grape acreage.

PASO POBLES (Spanish for "Pass of Oaks") is a turn-of-the 19th Century town, founded in 1889. The Chumash Indians prized what they called "Heaven's Spot" for all the thermal springs there. Even today, the Paso Robles Inn sits atop such a spring. Franciscan friars also partook of the springs as they travelled through the region on their way to found more missions.

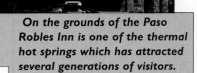

On the grounds of the *Paso Robles Inn* is one of the thermal hot springs which has attracted several generations of visitors.

The town square is the center of community life as it has been since Rancho Paso de Robles was created by a land grant in 1884.

Since the railroads brought out pioneering farmers, Paso Robles had become an agricultural area noted for its nearby ranches. Since the 1960s, it has become increasingly important in the Central Coast's wine industry and continues to add vineyard acreage as well as to house tasting rooms. Several antique shops, restaurants and businesses surrounding the town square cater to locals and visitors alike.

PASO ROBLES

In 1982, Arciero Vineyards/EOS Estate Winery, now with over 700 acres and production at 160,000 cases, pioneered the planting of several premium Italian varietals.

ARCIERO

DOCE ROBLES

Three lazy German Shepherds, Duchess, Syrah & Ellie greet visitors outside Doce Robles Winery. Inside is Grayson the cat, who often spends the daylight hours curled up in a basket on the end of the tasting bar. To complete the menagerie, there is Trickem the horse, but he's not kept in the tasting room.

From 1973 to 1977 Gary Eberle and Cliff Giacobine planted 700 acres, including the first modern commercial acreage of Syrah in the state, and established Estrella River Winery, the largest winery in the area.

Although Eberle provided Syrah plant material from that vineyard to many winemakers in the California, Rhone varietals did not form an important part of Paso Robles' identity until 1989. That year, the Perrin family established their international joint venture, Tablas Creek Vineyard in the limestone hills of the Adelaida region northwest of town. With 80 acres planted to the traditional varieties of Chateauneuf du Pape, Tablas Creek imported exclusive clonal material from the Rhone Valley, and made those clones available to other interested growers around the State. As a result, in addition to being a top producer of premium Rhone wines, Tablas Creek has evolved into a full-fledged vine nursery supplying cuttings of Rhone varietals to wineries all over California.

NEBBIOLO

The German name "Eberle" translates to "small boar", and a bronze boar greets every guest who visit the winery. The statue is the 93rd replica of the original bronze Porcellino cast by Tacca in 1620, the original of which can be found in the straw market in Florence, Italy.

Eberle Winery has 16,000 square feet of underground caves located below the winery to create the perfect place to age their wine.

EBERLE

Recognizing the area's unique yet very diverse terroir, the 614,000-acre Paso Robles AVA and 6,400-acre York Mountain AVA were established in 1983. In 1988, J. Lohr, whose winery owns over 1,900 acres of vineyards in the area and produces 400,000 cases annually, expanded into Paso Robles to focus on Cabernet Sauvignon, Merlot, Syrah and other red varietals. Meridian was also established then with 3,500 vineyard acres in California and annual production at 1.1 million cases, the largest of Paso Robles AVA wineries.

Due to the intense varietal character of wine grapes grown in this diverse appellation, Paso Robles Cabernet Sauvignon wines consistently garner national and international acclaim, including, among others, J. Lohr Vineyards and Wines, Treana Winery, Adelaida Cellars, and Chateau Margene.

Since 1989, Paso Robles has seen an explosion of Rhone varieties. It also has the largest acreage of Syrah, Viognier and Rousanne. Acres planted under Rhone varieties jumped from fewer than 100 acres in 1994 to more than 2,000 in 2005.

During that time, at least 10 wineries focusing on Rhone varieties were established. Paso Robles-based "Hospice du Rhone Festival", the largest celebration of Rhone wines in the world, is attended each year by 3,000 enthusiasts. In the last six years, the number of wineries in Paso Robles Wine Country has doubled to 100 mostly due to an influx of boutique and small family owned vineyards and wineries. The result is that many young boutique wineries are quickly gaining recognition and a following for their innovative and proprietary Paso Robles blends of Bordeaux, Rhone and Zinfandel varietals, including L'Aventure, Linne Calodo Cellars, Anglim Cellars, Halter Ranch Vineyard, Midnight Cellars, Pipestone Vineyards, Villicana Winery and Wild Coyote, among many others.

LONE MADRONE

P
A
S
O

R
O
B
L
E
S

MERIDIAN

Inland on Highway 46, Paso Robles is a cross-roads of agricultural activity, noted for its almond orchards and for its 150 vineyards. North in San Miguel is Mission San Miguel Arcangel (1797),16th of the 21 Missions in California, known for its well-preserved wall murals. Also the Caledonia Adobe (1850), once a stage stop and saloon, is preserved here.

MARTIN & WEYRICH

VILLA TOSCANA

TOBIN JAMES

BIANCHI

After searching throughout California for the finest terroir, in 2000 Bianchi chose property situated on a gentle rise with a commanding view looking west over undulating vineyards dotted with ancient oaks. The winery rises above a waterfall fed lake, and the building's glass walls take advantage of the peaceful surroundings from every angle. Cabernet Sauvignon, Zinfandel, Syrah and Merlot are planted in the winery's sloping vineyards. "Signature" wines are made from Edna Valley Chardonnay, Paso Robles Merlot, Sauvignon Blanc and others including Sangiovese, and Italian varietal called Refosco.

Built in 1994 at the site of an old stagecoach stop, Tobin James Cellars still has an old-fashioned western 1860 Brunswick mahogany bar complete with brass rails. But here you 'belly up' for wine tasting. The property still has many wooden structuers and a classic water pump tower complete with blades turning in the wind.

MEMORIAL

Movie idols are often immortalized because they died young, and one of the most recognized of these "stars" was James Dean.

After a fast rise to stardom with three major roles in movie hits - "East of Eden", "Rebel Without a Cause" and "Giant" - James Dean had two Oscar nominations and was on his way.

But he was also on his way to a road race in Salinas (Monterey County), driving his 1955 Porsche 550 Spyder, when he and his passenger were hit by another car at the intersection of Highway 46 and Highway 41 in Cholame, near Paso Robles. It was September 30, 1955, he did not survive the crash at 24 years old.

Dean to this day personifies rebellious American youth, his good looks, sullen and cool image defies time.

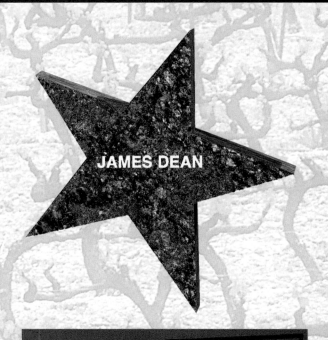

SAN SIMEON

SAN SIMEON is site of Sebastian's General Store (1852), a State Historical Landmark. Once a whaling village, the town is the gateway to Hearst Castle, and is a favorite for its beaches, which are known for the shells and moonstones found there. It is site of the Calif. Carvers Guild Museum. Inland is Lake Nacimiento, a resort area for windsurfing, waterskiing, fishing and camping. Ragged Point is rugged coastline at its wildest. South of the Point is Piedras Blancas Lighthouse (1874) reaching 110 ft (34 m) and still warning of the dangerous reefs below.

HEARST CASTLE, called by the romantic name "La Cuesta Encantada", is the enchanting hilltop retreat which once belonged to newspaper publisher William Randolph Hearst.

Now a State Historical Monument, moguls and movie stars of the 1920s and 30s visited the 'Castle' at Hearst's invitation. It took 28 years to complete the 165 rooms, vast European art and antique collection, exquisite pools and 127 acres (52 hectares) of gardens. The architecture embraces a Mediterranean style, and much of the Castle's elements were imported from Europe.

Bus tours now make the journey from the Highway below up to the entrance of the 127 acre estate.

MOVIE STARS

Reservations are required for the various tour packages. An iWerks Theatre in the Visitors Center features surround-sound and stories of the Castle's conception and construction. Four day-tours and one evening tour are available. Entrance to the hilltop area is only in conjunction with an official tour. Reservations: (800) 444-4445.

Encircled by fog, the "Castle" has 56 bedrooms and 61 bathrooms.

Upon climbing the stairs in front of La Cuesta Encantada, visitors' first view is impressive - the Neptune Pool glimmers in the sunlight.

A decorative frieze depicting actors from ancient cultures stands as a reminder of the many "Hollywood" guests who visited The Ranch, among them Charlie Chaplin, Greta Garbo, Gary Cooper and Clark Gable.

CENTRAL COAST TOWNS

OCEANO was an early Chumash Indian settlement, but after the railroads brought settlers in the 1890's, the town evolved as a nudist and artist colony during the 1930s. People no longer pursue this philosophy, rather one of the main attractions now is camping on the beach or riding All Terrain Vehicles on nearby Oceano Dunes State Recreation Area.

ATASCADERO, founded as a "utopia" in 1913, is site of the Charles Paddock Zoo featuring many species of wild cats, alligators, monkeys and bears. Outlet shopping is at Atascadero Factory Outlets. Make a stop at old Pozo Saloon (Hwy 58) on the way to Santa Margarita Lake, popular with locals for boating, fishing, kayaking, bird watching, hiking and equestrian trails. It is also a good spot to observe bald eagles.

CAYUCOS, favorite of surfers and fishermen, also has a number of antique shops. New Year's Day brings swimmers for the annual Polar Bear Dip.

 Quaint downtowns and relics of the past are abundant as are hiking and biking trails. Many towns, such as Atascadero are not only gateways to wine country, but have many festivals throughout the year.

CAMBRIA, site of dairy farms in the 1860s, is now home to many artists, art galleries and boutiques. Harmony (population 18) has a wedding chapel, artist's shops, and a winery.

MISSION SAN MIGUEL

Mission San Miguel had no bell tower, its 2,000 lb. bell rang out from a wooden platform in front of the mission and now sits in its own campanario behind the Church. The Mission has an annual fiesta on the third Sunday in September to celebrate the Feast Day of its patron, Saint Michael, chief of the Archangels and Prince of the Heavenly Armies. 801 Mission St., San Miguel

Founded in 1797 by Father Lasuen to complete the mission chain from San Luis Obispo to Mission Dolores in San Francisco, Mission San Miguel was located in the Salinas Valley as a mid-point between the San Luis Obispo and San Antonio Missions. Under the direction of Esteban Munros, the Indians painted the walls and ceilings with ornate designs; and these original murals are today the best preserved in California.

CASTORO

JUSTIN

Mission San Miguel was well established in producing wines for the mission system. Over the centuries, however, the buildings have continually succumbed to earthquake damage.

Several mid- to large-size operations have been focusing on hospitality for their showcase wineries. In addition to their tasting facility, Justin's complex includes the Isosceles Center, Just Inn and Deborah's Room.

CARMODY McNIGHT

...impressive coastal waters ...of the nation, as well as dynamic cityscapes of ...an unerring eye and the patience to wait for exactly ...resulting in images that perfectly record a moment in time. ...in his photographic imagery is to give people a sense of place and inspiration.

His photographic images can be seen on calendars, posters, books, music CD's, advertisements, periodicals, annual reports, postcards and various souvenirs. Among the foregoing, he has been represented in National Geographic Traveler, Outdoor Photographer, PC Photo, Estates West, Where, and AAA magazines. Also to his credit, he has affiliated his photographic efforts with The Sierra Club, The Wilderness Society, Ford Motor Co., UCLA, Price Weber, Princess Cruises, Caesars Palace, and Paris Hotels.

Global Graphics' Maps of CALIFORNIA Regions:

FOLDED PAPER MAPS:

LOS ANGELES STREET (Scale 1:45,000)	0-918505-15-1
LOS ANGELES FREEWAY (Scale 1: 250,000)	0-918505-16-X
CALIFORNIA CENTRAL COAST	0-918505-57-7
CALIFORNIA SOUTHERN COAST & NO. BAJA	0-918505-56-9
CALIFORNIA ROAD (Scale 1:1,100,000)	0-918505-12-7
CALIFORNIA WINE MAP	0-918505-51-8

LAMINATED MAPS:

QUICK ACCESS CALIFORNIA	0-918505-20-8
QUICK ACCESS CALIFORNIA MISSIONS	0-918505-61-5
QUICK ACCESS LOS ANGELES & Hollywood	0-918505-17-8
QUICK ACCESS LOS ANGELES FREEWAYS	0-918505-19-4
QUICK ACCESS SANTA BARBARA/SAN LUIS OBISPO - PASO ROBLES WINE COUNTRY MAP	0-918505-63-1
QUICK ACCESS ROUTE 66	0-918505-40-2
QUICK ACCESS SO. CALIF. RECREATION	0-918505-30-5